CW00405527

John Radcliffe's bequests have changed the face of historical Oxford, and their effects live on. Green Templeton College Fellow David Cranston has performed a valuable service, in the tercentenary year of the Doctor's death, by showing how and why this came about. As the College views the 21st century physical evolution of Oxford University, from the commanding heights of the Radcliffe Observatory, it is salutary to reflect on how science, medicine, management and architecture have made use of this legacy, and continue to do so through our work in education, research and public service.

Professor Sir David Watson, Principal, Green Templeton College

Dr Cranston has written a biography, as intriguing as it is scholarly, of one of Oxford's most remarkable benefactors. The incalculable benefits to science, medicine and architecture of Dr Radcliffe's largesse 300 years ago live on to this day and are an eloquent testimony to the vital contribution made by visionary philanthropy to the mission of a university: education, scholarship, research and the public good.

Sir Ivor Crewe, The Master, University College

I am delighted as a physician to commend a book written by a surgeon about a physician. In 1960 I had the good fortune to benefit from one of John Radcliffe's many acts of generosity to Oxford University. Holding a John Radcliffe Medical Travelling Fellowship, I spent a year at Harvard as part of my training to become a Consultant Neurologist. In the 18th century, Radcliffe Medical Fellows commonly went to the European centres of medical excellence, such as Bologna in Italy. That wise and robust sage, Dr Samuel Johnson, remarked that they and their patients might benefit more if they visited underdeveloped parts of the world such as South America, to study treatments and drugs outside Britain and Europe. Had they taken his advice, we might have benefited two centuries earlier from a wide range of drugs discovered in South America, such as curare.

Sir Roger Bannister

John Radcliffe
and his
Legacy to Oxford

John Radcliffe
and his
Legacy to Oxford

David Cranston
Illustrated by Valerie Petts

First published 2013 by

www.wordsbydesign.co.uk

ISBN: 978-1-909075-18-4

Portrait of John Radcliffe used with the permission
of the Oxford University Hospitals NHS Trust
Image of John Radcliffe's cane reproduced
with the permission of the Royal College of Physicians
All original illustrations © Valerie Petts (www.valeriepetts.co.uk)

Further copies of this book, as well as details of other publications and services, are available from

www.wordsbydesign.co.uk

David Cranston *completed his medical training in Bristol and worked in Exeter and Bath before coming to Oxford for post-graduate doctoral research. He is a Fellow of the Royal College of Surgeons of England and is currently Consultant Urological Surgeon in the Oxford University Hospitals NHS Trust, Associate Professor of Surgery in the Nuffield Department of Surgical Science and a Fellow of Green Templeton College, Oxford. Outside medicine he serves as a licenced lay minister in the Church of England and is on the board of the Oxford Centre for Mission Studies.*

Valerie Petts *first started training as a lab technician in Professor Howard Florey's department in Oxford before working in clinical immunology research in London and Sydney and has now been painting full-time since about 1990. She has had numerous exhibitions in England and has also exhibited in Tokyo and Cape Town. She has illustrated five books including* Oxford Words and Watercolours, Consider England *and visitor's book for the National Trust.*

Foreword

In 2014 it will be 300 years since John Radcliffe died. David Cranston has produced a very neat record of Radcliffe, his work and the life and times around him. The book is beautifully illustrated by Valerie Petts with a number of watercolours of buildings in Oxford associated with Radcliffe. As he points out in his opening paragraph, the name of Radcliffe is known by everybody in Oxford or visiting Oxford. For as a result of his benefactions we have the Radcliffe Library, the Radcliffe Camera and, up until recently, the Radcliffe Infirmary, to name but a few. Although the Radcliffe Infirmary is no more, there is the John Radcliffe Hospital, part of the Oxford University Hospitals NHS Trust, a major teaching hospital and ranked as the number one medical school in the world. However, very few people know much or indeed anything about John Radcliffe, and hence this book is a very readable source of information about a man who contributed so much to Oxford.

David Cranston gives us a lot of information about John Radcliffe the man, and I must say he does not come over as a very appealing individual, with a fierce temper and said to be extremely arrogant. However, he accrued a fortune from private practice fees as perhaps the leading physician in the country. One wonders how he achieved such renown and such a private practice at that time. But he did not believe in bleeding, cupping or purging, which undoubtedly resulted in the death of many very sick patients. Perhaps many of his successful cures were due not to his prescriptions but to the fact that he avoided these other conventional but potentially lethal approaches to treatment of the seriously ill patient. The author also gives us a glimpse of life in Oxford and London around this time which again puts John Radcliffe's work as a physician into perspective.

William Osler, Regius Professor of Medicine in Oxford, had intended in 1914 to celebrate the 200th anniversary of Radcliffe's death, but as he says in his introduction to the second edition of *The Gold Headed Cane* in 1915, there were other things of greater importance at the time, namely the First World War.

This small and very readable book is a worthy tribute to John Radcliffe on the occasion of the 300th anniversary of his death, and will be of great interest to anyone wishing to know more about this great benefactor to Oxford University.

Sir Peter J Morris AC FRS,
Emeritus Nuffield Professor of Surgery, University of Oxford.

ACKNOWLEDGEMENTS

My interest in John Radcliffe has grown over the years and, having given several lectures on him, it seemed appropriate to put something in writing in time for the 300th anniversary of his death in 2014.

I am very grateful to Professor Sir Peter Morris, not only for writing the Foreword to this book, but also for causing it to be written in the first place. He was responsible, as the Nuffield Professor of Surgery in 1983, for my appointment to Oxford as a Research Fellow in his department, and he has been on two subsequent appointment committees, which have allowed me to remain in Oxford.

Valerie Petts has transformed the book with her beautiful watercolours of some of the major Oxford landmarks associated with John Radcliffe. I am grateful too for the kind words of commendation written by Sir Ivor Crewe, Master of University College, the College to which John Radcliffe first came in 1665, and Professor Sir David Watson, Principal of Green Templeton College, who is currently the Guardian of the Radcliffe Observatory.

The year 2014 not only commemorates the 300th anniversary of John Radcliffe's death, but also the 60th Anniversary of a notable achievement by one of the Radcliffe Travelling Fellows, for on 6th May 1954 Roger Bannister became the first man to run a mile in under four minutes. I am grateful to him for his commendation and for his helpful advice over some aspects of the book.

Tony Gray has been most helpful as both editor and publisher through his company WORDS BY DESIGN, while my wife Rosie has been a constant source of support and encouragement in the ups and down of medical research and surgical life in Oxford over the last 30 years.

For Rosie

And in memory of
Grant Bates FRCS
1953-2011

Contents

Illustrations

Chapter 1: Radcliffe's World

Few people can come to Oxford without hearing of the name of Dr John Radcliffe, but not many people could tell you much about him. Yet his name lives on all around the city in the John Radcliffe Hospital, the Radcliffe Camera, the Radcliffe Observatory, and for over two centuries, until its closure in 2007, the old Radcliffe Infirmary.

But who was this man, the most famous physician of his day, who left so much to Oxford?

John Radcliffe was born in Wakefield. There is no doubt about his place of birth, close to what is now the Cathedral church, but the date of his birth is less clear, and it is of interest to note that he never seemed to be sure about his age. He was born in either 1650 or 1652. JB Nias, in his sketch of Radcliffe's life, mentions a letter shown to him by Sir William Osler (Regius Professor of Medicine in Oxford at the beginning of the twentieth century) from a man in Wakefield who stated that a child born to Radcliffe's parents in 1650 died in infancy and then, as was often done, the same name of John was then bestowed on the next child born. If this were true, it would seem that 1652 is the more likely date of his birth. He died on All Saints' Day, 1 November 1714 at the (probable) age of 62. He was regarded by many of his contemporaries as 'the Aesculapius of his age', taking that name from the renowned Greek god of medicine and healing.

John Radcliffe's grandfather, Rev. Roger Radcliffe, was curate of Wakefield in the early years of the seventeenth century, later becoming vicar of Horbury in West Yorkshire and subsequently

Dean of Doncaster. He died in 1651 and is buried in Wakefield . John Radcliffe's father, George, was an attorney and Governor of the Wakefield House of Correction, founded for the purpose of keeping down the numbers of 'beggars, rogues and dissolute people' within the West Riding of Yorkshire. The building was also used for the temporary housing of those captured by the press-gangs of the Royal Navy which were used to take men into the Navy, often by force, as a means of crewing British warships.

Radcliffe's initial education was at Wakefield Grammar School, where his father was also a governor. The school had been founded by a charter from Queen Elizabeth I in 1591 at the request of leading citizens in Wakefield. In John Radcliffe's day it was situated in pleasant grounds, 'a bowshot on the north from the Church', and it was based on the reading of Latin and Greek authors. It was said to be as famous as Westminster, Winchester and Eton, and among its other pupils was John Potter who became Regius Professor of Divinity in Oxford and subsequently was enthroned as Archbishop of Canterbury in 1737. The boys at Wakefield were expected to speak in Latin, although whether or not it was possible to enforce this is difficult to say. Nevertheless, as a physician John Radcliffe would have had good cause to retain his understanding of these languages throughout his life. Although he had no particular leaning towards classical learning, his results were sufficiently impressive for his parents to consider sending him to Oxford. Here, University College was the obvious choice as it had links with Yorkshire and the Freestone Foundation which supported scholars from a number of Yorkshire schools, including Wakefield Grammar School.

Little more is known about Radcliffe's time in Wakefield, although one story exists of his return to the place of his birth at the age of 21. By this time he was already a Fellow of Lincoln College Oxford and he had gone back to Wakefield with two Oxford friends. One afternoon they had gone to listen to Oliver Heywood, a well-respected Presbyterian preacher. Heywood describes the scene of 1674 in his diary:

In the afternoon many came, among whom was a wild young scholar, one Radcliffe. He hearkened diligently, yet on Monday night he helped down liquor with his companions with mimicry of my sermon and the delivery of it.

He does not record how good the mimicry was.

Chapter 2: Radcliffe at Oxford

Radcliffe matriculated at Oxford on 23 March 1665 and remained there until 1684. He entered University College which, along with Balliol and Merton, are the oldest of Oxford's colleges, established between 1249 and 1264 – although there is some dispute as to which was the first. His entry in the University records states that he was 15 but the Wakefield Parish Church register seems to show that he was only 13, which would fit with a birth date of 1652.

The Oxford colleges had initially arisen through the gradual agglomeration of independent institutions in the city of Oxford. The first academic houses were monastic halls, although of the dozens that were established in Oxford during the twelfth to fifteenth centuries, none survived the Reformation. The present-day Dominican Hall of Blackfriars is a descendant of the original one founded in 1221, and is therefore sometimes described as heir to the oldest tradition of teaching in Oxford. Eight different titles are in use for the heads of colleges: Principal, Master, Warden, President, Provost, Dean, Rector and Regent.

The Oxford to which Radcliffe came in 1665 was recovering from the Civil War (1642-51) which had been fought to ensure that an English monarch could not govern without Parliament's consent. Oxford had been occupied by Charles I during the Civil War, and King Charles assembled the Oxford Parliament in January 1644 with the purpose of fighting the Royalist war campaign. Oxford was the centre of the King's (Cavalier) cause and became the headquarters of the King's forces. This had both advantages and disadvantages, as most of the citizens were undoubtedly favourable to the Roundhead

University College Quad

cause but also enjoyed the financial rewards of supplying the court and garrison of the King. The position of Oxford gave King Charles I the strategic advantage of controlling the Midland counties. However, the dangers of the city increased as opposition grew. The King was resident at Christ Church and the Queen at Merton (the Queen's room remains), with access being gained to each other through Corpus Christi. The mills in Osney became a powder factory and New College the magazine. At New Inn Hall the college plate that the King had requisitioned and taken from the colleges was melted down into 'Oxford Crowns' and a gibbet was erected at Carfax. College life continued, albeit on a restricted and disturbed scale.

Oxford had subsequently surrendered to Fairfax, commander of the Parliamentarians (Roundheads), after the King had escaped to the North. Charles I was captured, tried, convicted, and executed for high treason in 1649.

Following this, the monarchy was abolished and the Commonwealth of England was ruled by Parliament until Cromwell became Lord Protector of England in 1653. Oliver Cromwell, who initially was second-in-command to Fairfax, had been elected Chancellor of Oxford University in 1650. A number of senior academics in Oxford refused to submit to Parliament and were replaced, but due to Oliver Cromwell's support, the numbers in the University increased and academic life and rights were restored. The prevailing tone and teaching in Oxford was on Puritan lines, and the morals and behaviour of the undergraduates were carefully guarded. Following the death of Cromwell in 1658 and the failure of his son as Lord Protector, the monarchy was eventually restored in 1660 and Charles II, son of Charles I, ascended the throne. The restoration was accompanied by social change. Puritanism lost its momentum and one Earl, Wilmot, supposedly said of the new King:

We have a pretty witty King
And whose word no man relies on,
He never said a foolish thing,
And never did a wise one.

To which Charles supposedly said, "That's true, for my words are my own, but my actions are those of my ministers."

Charles II transferred the Court and Parliament to Oxford again in 1665 due to the Great Plague, and it remained there until January 1666. Radcliffe would have been there to see it. This was the last major epidemic of the bubonic plague or Black Death to occur in England. It had begun in Europe in 1347 and finally ended in 1750. Caused by the *Yersinia pestis* bacterium and transmitted through the bite of an infected flea, the Great Plague killed an estimated 100,000 people – about 20% of London's population. It was called the 'Black Death', not primarily to describe the late-stage sign of the disease, in which the sufferer's skin would blacken due to haemorrhages and gangrene below the skin, but more likely to refer to blackness of mood in the terror and gloom of the events.

The intellectual life in Oxford was buzzing with new ideas and new people at the time. John Wilkins was Warden of Wadham College. He was a clergyman and brother-in-law of Oliver Cromwell, and one of the few people to have been head of an Oxford and a Cambridge college. As one of the founders of the Royal Society he attracted a number of rising stars, including Thomas Sydenham, Robert Boyle and a young man who had been appointed Professor of Astronomy in Oxford, but was to leave his mark on England as one of the greatest architects the country has ever known – Christopher Wren.

Thomas Sydenham was an English physician who fought for Parliament throughout the English Civil War and, at its end, resumed his medical studies at Oxford. He became the undisputed master of the English medical world and was known as 'The English Hippocrates' after the ancient Greek physician of the fifth century BC who was acclaimed as the father of western medicine. Among Sydenham's many achievements was the discovery of a disease, Sydenham's Chorea, also known as St Vitus' Dance. This is characterised by rapid, uncoordinated jerking movements affecting primarily the face, feet and hands, usually resulting from a childhood bacterial infection.

Robert Boyle was also at Oxford. He was a natural philosopher, chemist, physicist and inventor, who was also noted for his writings in theology. He is best known for Boyle's Law, describing the relationship between the pressure and volume of a gas. Boyle later became President of the Royal Society, and Louis Pasteur said that it was by pondering Boyle's comments on fermentation that he was first moved to make his discoveries in the field of bacteriology.

Christopher Wren, as well as being Professor of Astronomy, was responsible for designing the Sheldonian Theatre which was being built while Radcliffe was an undergraduate. It cost £14,000 and was paid for by Dr Gilbert Sheldon, then Archbishop of Canterbury. Wren also rebuilt St Paul's Cathedral after the great Fire of London and many of the churches of the capital.

Another important Oxford thinker was John Locke, an English philosopher and physician regarded as one of the most influential of Enlightenment thinkers. An Oxford anatomist by the name of William Petty was also well-known in Oxford, but perhaps best remembered as the doctor who resuscitated Anne Green, a lady who had been hung for the murder of her illegitimate child. He received the body after the hanging, as it was the custom for medical students to practise dissection on the bodies of executed criminals. However, she was found to be alive and, with Thomas Willis and other colleagues, Petty revived her. She subsequently married, had a further three children and lived for another 15 years.

Ten years later while Radcliffe was studying medicine the Ashmolean Museum was founded, 'to house all manner of rare beasts, fowls and birds, shells and stones'. The collection was given to the University by Elias Ashmole, having been assembled by his father, and the building became the first public museum in England.

However, classical scholarship and scientific research was by no means the only pursuit that Oxford fellows and students engaged in. Since the Puritan days, morals had lapsed. Drunken heads, drunken fellows and drunken students were all too common, along with gambling, dicing and brawling. So much so that, 'some hesitated in sending their sons to Oxford for fear of corruption'.

Such was the Oxford to which Radcliffe came in 1665. He arrived at University College and came under the care of the senior fellow and tutor, Obadiah Walker. Walker was a convinced Royalist who had been ejected from his fellowship in 1648, went abroad and was drawn to the Roman Catholic Church, making his views known on the accession of the James II (brother of Charles II) who was also a Catholic. He was eventually elected as Master of University College in 1676. With the fall of the King in 1688 (who fled the country after producing a Catholic heir, and was deemed to have abdicated), Walker left the University, spent some time imprisoned in the Tower of London, was eventually released but lived the remainder of his life in poverty. He was cared for by Radcliffe who sent him a new suit of clothes every year and a dozen bottles of the richest Canary (a sweet fortified wine made in the Canary Islands since the fifteenth century) which was the drink of choice for aristocrats, writers and merchants. Radcliffe sent it to Walker to, 'support his drooping spirits', and he ended up living with Radcliffe and eventually died in 1698.

Radcliffe studied Latin, Greek, Aristotle's logic, grammar and metaphysics for his degree. He had to attend certain university lectures and 'disputations', but these were said to be formal and uninspiring, and attendance was often very slack. He is said to have acquitted himself well for his Bachelor's and subsequent Master's degree, and apparently his performance was greeted with great applause.

He was elected a senior scholar at University College in 1667 and to a Fellowship at Lincoln in 1670. At Lincoln he was lecturer in logic in 1671 and lecturer in philosophy in 1672. His father had died by this time and his mother apparently increased his allowance, enabling him to take up the study of physics and also courses in anatomy, chemistry and botany.

Licences for the practice of medicine and surgery were issued by the University of Oxford on the basis of the candidate having taken his Master of Arts (MA) and having spent three years in medicine, including compulsory attendance of the Regius Professor of

Medicine's lectures on Hippocrates and Galen twice a week at 8.00am.

The teaching of medicine in the seventeenth century still relied heavily on the work of the ancient physicians. Hippocrates, born on the island of Cos in 460 BC, founded the Hippocratic School of Medicine and was the first to establish medicine as a profession. He was also responsible for the Hippocratic Oath (see Appendix), an ethical statement on the practice of medicine which is still used in some medical schools to this day. Galen, born in AD 192, was a prominent Roman of Greek background coming from Pergamum in modern-day Turkey. A physician, surgeon and philosopher, he was one of the most accomplished of all medical researchers of antiquity. Galen contributed greatly to the understanding of anatomy, pathology, pharmacology and physiology, as well as philosophy and logic. He was the personal physician to several of the Roman emperors, including Marcus Aurelius.

Medical science in Radcliffe's day had already begun to embark on modern development. William Harvey was a leading physician and the first to describe the circulation of the blood in his classic work *De Motu Cordis*. He published his work in 1628, opening it with a dedication to King Charles I to whom he was physician-in-ordinary, accompanying him on all his travels. During the Civil War Harvey remained with the king and helped the wounded, and on several occasions he protected the king's children. Harvey followed Charles to Oxford, where he was made 'Doctor of Physic' in 1642, and later became Warden of Merton College in 1645. He remained there until the city's surrender, moving to London the following year.

Radcliffe needed some knowledge of anatomy and was expected to take part in disputations in the medical school. The degree of Bachelor of Medicine and Doctor of Medicine (BM and DM) was given by the University, but only a handful would take the degree of BM every year and only two or three the DM. It was generally thought that the training was not good and that real students of medicine looked elsewhere to further the education that Oxford lacked, often travelling to universities overseas.

Radcliffe himself admitted that his medical knowledge was derived largely from Dr Thomas Willis, an eminent Oxford physician whose major interests were in the brain and nervous system. He gave his name to the Circle of Willis, an arterial *anastomosis* (the connection of two blood vessels) within the brain, and his work on the anatomy of the brain, illustrated by Sir Christopher Wren, became a classic. Radcliffe was also able to wander through the Botanic Garden next to Magdalen College and obtain the odd tutorial on plants and herbs from the curator, but it appears he studied this in an irregular manner.

In 1666, a year after Radcliffe came to Oxford, the Great Fire destroyed much of London. Raging from Sunday 2 September to Wednesday 5 September, it gutted the medieval City of London inside the old Roman City Wall. Sparing Westminster and Charles II's Palace of Whitehall, it consumed 13,200 houses, 87 parish churches and St Paul's Cathedral, destroying the homes of 70,000 of the city's 80,000 inhabitants. The death toll is unknown but thought to have been small although it is possible that the deaths of poor and middle-class people were not recorded. News of this would have been the talk of Oxford where Radcliffe was embarking on his second year of studies under a new Vice-Chancellor, Dr John Fell. Fell insisted on regular attendance at lectures and made examinations stricter than they had been. Very enthusiastic and self-assertive, he was not universally popular, as the following ditty records:

I do not like thee Dr Fell,
The reason why I cannot tell,
But this I only know too well,
I do not like thee Dr Fell.

Radcliffe was not considered a scholar by his contemporaries. On one occasion when Dr Bathurst, the President of Trinity, called on him in his room in Lincoln, he was surprised to see so few books in his study. Radcliffe pointed to a few vials, a skeleton and an herbal (a book containing the names of plants with information on their medical use), and is said to have remarked, "This is Radcliffe's library." Late in life when visiting his successor, Dr Richard Mead, he noticed Dr Mead reading Hippocrates in Greek. "I have never read Hippocrates in my life," Radcliffe is quoted as saying. The young diplomat is reported as answering, "You, sir, have no occasion. You are Hippocrates himself." Perhaps Mead was after a good reference! Radcliffe may have been more widely read than these illustrations suggest, and certainly William Pittis, who wrote his biography shortly after his death, suggested that his conversation with friends and acquaintances could be very wide-ranging, pointing to a general knowledge belied by first impressions.

Radcliffe had to resign his Fellowship at Lincoln in 1677 when he was obliged to take Holy Orders if he wished to remain at the college. He applied for a faculty to allow him to remain as a Fellow, but his bluntness and criticism of others, together with his quarrels with the Rector, meant that that was refused. He left Lincoln and took rooms in the town to continue his practice. He left nothing to Lincoln in his will, but did contribute £10 towards a fine chestnut panelling for the senior common room in 1684, which apparently was twice as much as any of the other fellows had donated.

The Radcliffe Coat of Arms
(see page 54)

Chapter 3: Doctor in Oxford

Radcliffe began his medical practice in Oxford on obtaining his BM degree in 1675, and displayed the characteristics which marked his whole career.

He was independent in his treatment, often abusive to patients and was not concerned about antagonising his more conservative medical colleagues to whom he was often overbearing and insolent. What was said of him in later life was true of the whole of his medical career:

> *Two of a trade – where one of the two is a John Radcliffe – can never agree.*

Some of his contemporaries thought that 'all Radcliffe's cures were performed by guesswork'. He quarrelled with the two leading apothecaries (pharmacists of the day) in Oxford who did not like his methods, but his astute diagnosis and new methods of treatment worked. This meant that most of the apothecaries came round to his way of thinking and were eager to dispense for him. Smallpox was a common disease in Oxford and the surrounding countryside at the time. Many died from it, and those who did recover were often disfigured for life. Radcliffe's treatment was novel for the time and produced many successes. He insisted on his patients having an abundance of fresh air and cooling emulsions, rather than shutting them up in a confined space and bleeding them, thus 'rescuing more than 100 from attacks of death'. This together with his emphasis on personal hygiene and common sense meant that while he was feared as a man, he became trusted as a doctor.

His greatest success in Oxford came with the treatment of Lady Spencer, an ancestor of Princess Diana, whose husband Sir Thomas was lord of the nearby Manor of Yarnton. He had been ill for a number of years, although it is not recorded what ailed him. Lady Spencer's son-in-law came to hear of Radcliffe's success and persuaded her to call him in. Radcliffe came and prescribed, and within three weeks Sir Thomas was fitter than he had been for many years. As a result of this success, Radcliffe found his services in demand from many noble families in the area. Sir Thomas subsequently died in 1685 at the age of 47 and the marble tomb erected in his memory by his wife can be seen today in Yarnton parish church.

In Radcliffe's day uroscopy, or diagnosis by study of the urine, was well-known, and a number of paintings by famous artists show a physician holding up a flask containing urine to the light before pronouncing judgement on the patient's diagnosis. On one occasion in Oxford, a lady came to Radcliffe with a bottle of her sick husband's urine asking him for a diagnosis of his disease and a prescription to treat it.

"Where is he?" cried the doctor. "In a sick bed four miles off," she replied. "And that's his water no doubt?" "Yes," she replied. "What is his trade?" asked Radcliffe. "He is a boot maker," she answered. "Very well, mistress," cried Radcliffe, and taking the urinal he emptied it into the chamber pot and then filled it with his own urine and dismissed her with this advice: "Take this with you home to your husband and if he will undertake to fit me with a pair of boots by the sight of my water, I'll make no question of prescribing for his distemper [see Appendix] by a view of his."

'Like to a queen in pride of place, she wears
The splendour of a crown in Radcliffe's dome.'

(see page 53)

CHAPTER 4: MOVE TO LONDON

Having made his name in Oxford and established a wide reputation, Radcliffe decided in 1684, at the age of 32, to move to London and there seek his fortune as a London physician. His rise to fame was rapid, partly due to his force of character and diagnostic acumen. However, his move to London may have been connected with a state visit paid to Oxford in the spring of 1683 by James Duke of York (later James II) in the company of his second wife and unmarried daughter, the Princess Anne, whom Radcliffe probably met through Obadiah Walker, Master of University College.

James came to the throne in 1685, succeeding his brother Charles II, and reigning as James II of England and Ireland, and as James VII of Scotland. Although James remained a staunch adherent to the Roman Catholic faith, his two surviving daughters, Mary and Anne, were brought up as Protestants. Another six of his children had died in infancy.

Princess Anne had been married in the summer of 1683 to Prince George of Denmark and a home was provided for her in Whitehall by her uncle, King Charles II. In 1686 when Radcliffe had been in London for two years, Princess Anne's father, now King James II, selected Radcliffe as her physician. She had already lost three children when Radcliffe took over her care. The fourth child William survived, the only one of her 17 children to survive infancy.

When William Duke of Gloucester was four years old, he had a serious illness but Radcliffe saved his life and was presented with 1,000 guineas from the princess. However, he upset her when he refused to accompany her to Nottingham after James II's abdication in 1688. In 1694 she was unwell and sent for Radcliffe, who at the time was engaged in drinking with his friends and delayed going. When a second messenger arrived, he said with an oath that, "Her Highness's distemper was nothing but the vapours and she was in as good estate of health as any woman breathing." This was reported to the princess who dismissed him as Royal Physician.

In 1687 Radcliffe was admitted by royal favour as one of the original Fellows in the Royal College of Physicians, although he was to have a strained relationship with the College for the rest of his life. On one occasion he is reported as saying to the President of the College that the whole of medicine could be put on a sheet of notepaper, to which the President replied, "As far as you know it, it certainly could."

At the end of the seventeenth century the apothecaries did much general practice, but remained subordinate to the physician. The usual custom was for the apothecary to see the patient and then go to a coffee house where he found the physician that he wished to consult. He described the symptoms and received a 'bill' or prescription from the doctor, written in Latin with directions as to what should be done for treatment. After receiving the prescription, the apothecary made up the medicines, then went back to the patient and administered the prescribed medicine himself. If bleeding was required, the barber surgeon was called in, and when cupping was necessary, a cupper was called. The physician never saw the patient except in serious cases. The standard fee to be paid to the physician for his prescriptions and advice was 10s 6d. The apothecary's business was very lucrative. Dandridge, who worked with Radcliffe, was said to have accumulated £50,000 during his working lifetime.

Sometimes the apothecaries carried out their own general practice and began to prescribe on their own responsibility, although they were still meant to be subordinate to the physicians. One popular ditty describes them in the following way:

So modern 'pothecaries taught the art,
By Doctors' bills, to play the Doctor's part:
Bold in the practice of mistaken rules,
Prescribe, apply, and call their Masters fools.

The practice of bloodletting, or phlebotomy, dates back to antiquity. The followers of Hippocrates in the fifth century BC strongly believed in bleeding patients, and it is likely that this was done in Egyptian times and probably even before that. There were complex theories as to why bloodletting was necessary and why it worked. An early theory was that an imbalance in the four bodily humours – blood, phlegm, black bile, and yellow bile – was postulated as the need for bloodletting [see Appendix]. Virtually every known medical condition at one time or another was treated by bloodletting. As one can imagine, treating an anaemic patient by removing even more blood was not the best of ideas and many died as a result.

The great tenet of medicine, *Primum non nocere* (First do no harm), has been abused down the centuries, often from ignorance but sometimes for personal gain, and no age has been free from abuse.

Wet cupping referred to placing a cup over the wound as a receptacle for the blood. There were often suction devices attached to the cup to allow the removal of blood. At times 'dry cupping' was used. This technique entailed creating suction in a heated cup placed over the skin without cutting the skin. The cup was placed on the skin and suction was created as it cooled. The skin then became engorged, presumably with evil humours that could improve health by coming to the surface.

The usual round of a physician in Radcliffe's day was to rise late, and then, clothed in dressing gown, drink his morning chocolate followed by tea and toast. The visiting barber would come and shave him, and then he was dressed according to strict professional etiquette – a wig (which could cost up to forty guineas), powdered every day, and a full coat of black or velvet possessing large cuffs

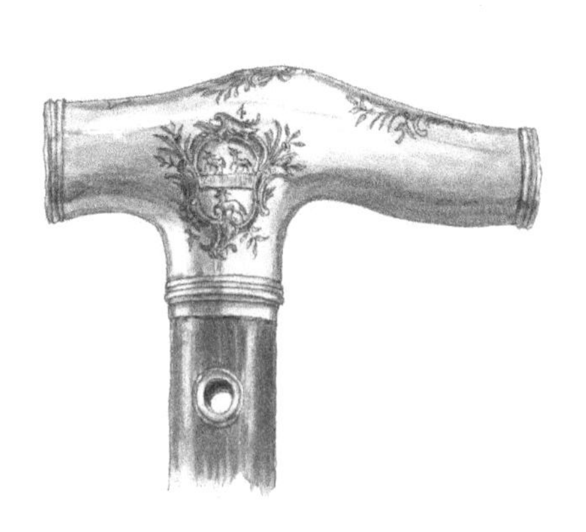

John Radcliffe's Cane

with plenty of buttons. The doctor would have a coach with two, four or six horses, depending on his importance. Before going out to visit patients or to sit in the coffee house, he would put on his three-cornered hat and take his professional cane. In winter he would usually have a fur muff for his hands to keep them warm before touching the patient. The chief business of the physician's day was concluded before dinner which began around 6.00pm. At dinner, lavish portions of food usually including many meat dishes were served. A typical meal might include pigeons, sirloin of beef, venison, leg of mutton, turkey, snipes, ducks, or partridge – all washed down with plenty of alcohol in the form of port or claret. After dinner there was much talking and further drinking with cards or dicing, or sometimes a trip to the theatre.

The cane was an essential part of a physician's professional attire, much as the stethoscope is today, and was probably derived from the snake-entwined staff of Aesculapius, which remains a symbol of medicine today. Aesculapius was the god of medicine and healing in ancient Greek religion. The serpent and the staff appear to have been separate symbols that were combined at some point in the development of the Aesculapius cult. The significance of the serpent has been interpreted in different ways: the shedding of its skin by the snake and its renewal symbolising rejuvenation, while the serpent could also symbolise the dual nature of the work of the physician, who deals with life and death, sickness and health. The ambiguity of the serpent as a symbol, and the contradictions it is thought to represent, reflect the ambiguity of the use of drugs, which can help or harm, something that is reflected in the meaning of the word *pharmakon*, which could mean either 'drug', 'medicine' or 'poison' in ancient Greek.

No doctor of note would be seen in public without his staff. It would have a heavy knob of silver or gold in which was an aromatic or vinaigrette preparation which the physician would hold to his nose and sniff whilst visiting the sick as protection from contagion and for neutralising foul odours. On entering, the physician might strike the cane upon the floor before applying the knob to his nostrils in order to keep foul smelling odours away. The entrance was designed to be dramatic and impress his audience!

A famous picture by William Hogarth in 1736 entitled 'The Company of Undertakers' caricatures twelve physicians consulting on the contents of a urinal, each sniffing the handles of their canes to protect themselves. The motto underneath reads:

Et Plurima Mortis Imago,
And many an image of death.

The passing on of a gold-headed cane from an older to a younger physician was a sign of high regard and affection, and became a common practice in the eighteenth century. Radcliffe passed his on to his successor, Richard Mead, and from him it went to Askew, Pitcairn and Baillie.

It is not clear when Radcliffe first acquired his gold-headed cane, but it later became the subject of a book written in 1827 by William MacMichael entitled, *The Gold Headed Cane*, in which he tells with great skill the story, from the cane's point of view, of its five masters, Radcliffe being the first.

He puts these words into the cane's mouth as it listens to the oration in the Royal College of Physicians where it came to lay in 1825 – after its last owner, Baillie, had died and his widow had given it to the College of Physicians:

I had passed through so many erudite hands, and had been present at so many grave consultations, that the language of the oration was familiar to me.... Formerly the entrée of palaces had been open to me and I had been freely admitted to the houses of the great and the rich; but now I was doomed to darkness and condemned to occupy a corner of the library.

In London, Radcliffe set up practice in Bow Street, Covent Garden. This was conveniently placed for Whitehall, Westminster and the residences of the wealthy city merchants. Much of London was still rural, including Oxford Street (or Oxford Road, as it was then called) which had hedges on either side, while in the fields around Regent Street and the meadows of Marylebone there was abundant pasture for cattle and game for sportsmen.

Often political attachments influenced a doctor's practice and it was said of Radcliffe that the Whigs employed him for his skill and the Tories for his politics (they were the two main political parties of the day). He had not been in town for more than a year before he was earning twenty guineas a day for his work, and indeed he would sometimes charge this amount to visit a single patient. If a patient sent a servant to him for advice, his charge was two guineas for the first visit, one for the second, two for the third, and so on.

It is difficult to work out the exact worth of this amount of money today and figures vary from £2,000 (using the retail price index) to £31,000 (using average earnings). However, for five shillings in 1690 (1/84 of Radcliffe's earnings) you could buy two days' labour from a craftsman in the building trade, and it would appear that the spending power of twenty guineas would be around £2,000 today. When in later years he left money to Oxford, it included a figure of £150 to cover the annual salary of a librarian.

He soon amassed a fortune and was persuaded by the actor Betterton to risk a speculative investment of £5,000 in a ship in a venture in the East Indies. The French captured the vessel and news was bought to Radcliffe of his loss. He seemed unconcerned and implied that he could make it good in a short period of time. Unfortunately, that was not true of Betterton who was subsequently reduced to poverty.

Radcliffe's next-door neighbour in Bow Street was Sir Godfrey Kneller, the leading portrait painter in England during the late seventeenth and early eighteenth centuries. Kneller was court painter to the British monarchs from Charles II to George I. He and Radcliffe became good friends and Kneller had a fine garden with rare flowers and exotic plants. A wall divided the gardens, and one day Radcliffe asked if a door could be made so that he could enjoy Kneller's garden. Kneller readily agreed and it was done. However, Radcliffe's servants abused the hospitality and damaged the garden, unreproved, it would seem, by the doctor. Eventually, Kneller, the courteous and patient man that he was, could stand it no more and bricked up the door. Radcliffe sent his footman round to Kneller's house with the message that, "Sir Godfrey could do what he liked with the door as long as he did not paint it." "Did my good friend Dr Radcliffe say so?" cried Sir Godfrey to the footman who hesitatingly delivered the message. "Then go back to him and tell him, after presenting my service to him, that I can take anything from him but physic."

Radcliffe was generally thought of as a good raconteur, although some found his conversation excessive. This is demonstrated in a few lines by one contemporary poet, Matthew Prior, who often spent evenings in Radcliffe's company:

I sent for Radcliffe, was so ill,
The other doctors gave me over;
He felt my pulse, prescribed his pill,
and I was likely to recover.
But when the Wit began to wheeze,
and wine had warmed the Politician,
Cured yesterday of my disease,
I died last night of my Physician.

The Radcliffe Infirmary

Chapter 5: Royal Consultations

In 1688 James II faced a crisis when his second wife Queen Mary, herself a Catholic, gave birth to a Catholic son, James Francis Edward Stuart.

After the birth of James II's son, the prospect of a Roman Catholic dynasty in the kingdoms was now likely. If James II had not had a son, the throne would have passed to his daughter Mary, a Protestant, the wife (and cousin) of William of Orange. Already troubled by the King's Catholicism and his close ties with France, key leaders of the Tories united with members of the opposition, the Whigs, and set out to resolve the crisis by inviting William of Orange to England to land an invasion army from the Netherlands. However, after two minor clashes in England, war was averted as James fled the country and was thus deemed to have abdicated after the Glorious Revolution of 1688.

William III and Mary II, both Protestants, became joint rulers in 1689. After the accession of William III to the throne, Radcliffe treated two of the king's friends and the king was so impressed that he gave Radcliffe 500 guineas and offered him the post of Court Physician. Although Radcliffe diplomatically declined this offer, the king, when ill, nevertheless called him in. MacMichael tells the story (from the cane's viewpoint) of one of these consultations:

> *It was the autumn of 1689 and my master, Dr Radcliffe had just returned from a distant journey to the country when an urgent message reached him at his house in Bow Street. Snatching me up he hurried for his carriage, and set off with all speed for Kensington House.*

The cane goes on to describe the drive to the house, the entrance and the suite of rooms through which they passed, stopping briefly as Radcliffe looked at the portrait of Dr Linacre, founder of the Royal College of Physicians (painted by Holbein), hanging in one of the rooms amongst the portraits of kings and queens of England and Scotland. The cane goes on:

> *On entering the sick chamber, a person of grave and solemn aspect, apparently about forty years of age, of a thin and weak body, brown hair and of middle stature, was seen sitting in an arm chair, and breathing with great difficulty. The naturally serious character of the king (for it was His Majesty William the Third) was rendered more melancholy by the distressing symptoms of an asthma, the consequences of the dregs of small-pox that had fallen on his lungs."*

The cane continues to describe how the king had been pressed by the Earls of Portland and Rockford to send for Radcliffe, despite the presence of two other physicians who were attending the king. Radcliffe told the King:

> *I must be plain with you, Sir: your case is one of danger, no doubt, but if you will adhere to my prescriptions, I will engage to do you good. The rheum (thin mucus discharge) is dripping on your lungs, and will be of fatal consequences to you, unless it be otherwise diverted.*

The other physicians were somewhat put out by Radcliffe, whose diagnosis and suggested remedy insinuated bad practice on their part. Nevertheless Radcliffe's view prevailed and the king recovered to such an extent that a few months later, in the summer of 1690, he fought and won the Battle of the Boyne when the deposed James II landed in Ireland and sought unsuccessfully to regain the throne.

In 1694 Radcliffe was also consulted at a late stage for the last illness of Queen Mary, but was unable to save her. He is reported as saying bluntly that her treatment had been wrong. Some blamed him for her death, but he was later exonerated when it was found that he was called in only when she was close to death from smallpox. Nevertheless William still consulted and employed Radcliffe for a while until the time when Radcliffe examined the king's swollen legs on one occasion and exclaimed, "Why, truly, I would not have your Majesty's two legs for your three kingdoms." This exhausted the king's patience with him and he was never officially consulted again.

He was called into treat the Duke of Beaufort who had smallpox and at the time was being treated by his grandmother with closed curtains and windows. He is said to have bundled her out of the room, opened the windows and let the fresh air in, and thus successfully treated the Duke who made a full recovery – to the overwhelming gratitude of the Duchess. On another occasion the Duchess of Marlborough asked Radcliffe to come to Cambridge to treat her son, the Marquis of Blandford, who was ill with smallpox. He said he could not leave his London patients, some of who were seriously ill, but gave directions for the Marquis' treatment. It was ignored and the Marquis died. Apparently he told the Duchess that the doctors had killed her son, although it is uncertain how true this was, and gossip in the clubs of London may have exaggerated some of these stories.

Radcliffe took a particular dislike to one colleague, a Dr Edward Hannes, also an Oxford man. Hannes was a very ambitious man who promoted himself by sending his footmen into town to put their heads into every carriage asking, as if it were a matter of life and death, whether Dr Hannes was within the carriage. Acting on these orders, one of his fellows, after looking into every carriage between Whitehall and the Royal Exchange, ran into Garraway's Coffee House (one of the great meeting places of the medical profession), asking, "Gentlemen, can your honours tell me if Dr Hannes is here?"

"Who wants Dr Hannes, fellow?" demanded Radcliffe, who happened to be there.

"Lord A and Lord B," came the reply.

"No, no my friend," responded the doctor slowly, "You are mistaken. Those Lords don't want your master – 'tis he who wants them."

Nevertheless, Hannes eventually became one of Queen Anne's physicians and was knighted by her in 1702.

Sir Hans Sloane was another famous London physician of the day and near-neighbour of Radcliffe when he moved to London. He was a great collector of natural history specimens and other items from around the world, and after his death the collection eventually became the beginnings of the British Museum and the Natural History Museum. In one of his travels to Jamaica, Sloane came across cocoa where the locals drank it mixed with water. He found it nauseating until he discovered that, mixed with milk, it became much more pleasant. When he returned to England he brought the chocolate recipe back with him and initially apothecaries sold it as medicine. A century later the Cadbury brothers were selling tins of Sloane's Drinking Chocolate. He was another of Queen Anne's physicians and became President of the Royal College of Physicians and later succeeded Sir Isaac Newton as president of the Royal Society. His name is commemorated in several places in London, including Sloane Square and Hans Road.

Radcliffe could be very generous if the occasion arose. On one occasion he received a letter from one Jonathan Savil who was under sentence of death. Savil confessed to having burgled Radcliffe's house and begged him to have his death sentence commuted to transportation. Radcliffe received the letter when his was drinking with friends in the Mitre Tavern in Fleet Street, and his drinking partners expected the messenger to be dismissed forthwith. However, Radcliffe was moved by the message and took Lord Granville into another room and asked him to intercede with the Queen. As a result, Savil was transported to Virginia where he did well and subsequently kept in touch with Radcliffe.

On another occasion, when a certain impoverished barrister by the name of William Nutley was taken ill and Radcliffe was called in, he found the man in a severe state of depression which was greatly increased by his substantial debts. Radcliffe sent round a purse of 200 sovereigns with a letter "To my dear Billy", saying that he had "never been so niggardly as to prefer mountains of gold to conversation of a person that gives gaiety to old age". He promised to send a further £300 but the young man continued drinking and died a few days later before the second gift arrived. Generous in large gifts, he could also be miserly with loose change. He was a bad loser at cards, and often sponged on his companions for small sums, saying that he hated to change a guinea because it slipped away so fast.

After Mary died in 1694, William ruled alone until his death in 1702. William and Mary were childless and were ultimately succeeded by Mary's younger sister, Anne, also a daughter of James II. Queen Anne came to the throne in March 1702, and reigned for twelve years until her death in August 1714.

When Anne acceded to the throne on the death of her brother-in-law, William of Orange, she refused to reinstate Radcliffe in view of the way he had treated her previously, although he was often consulted behind the scenes.

In 1700, two years before her accession, Radcliffe was summoned at a late stage to Windsor to Anne's son, the eleven-year-old Duke of Gloucester, whose life Radcliffe had saved when he was four years old. He was reported to have said in a fit of temper to the other physicians who had been treating him, including Hannes, "You have destroyed him, and you may finish him for I will not prescribe."

However, Radcliffe's report of the case, now in the Radcliffe Science Library, shows he did everything possible to save the prince's life (see Appendix).

Who knows what would have happened had he been called in earlier? Had the prince survived he would have been the natural successor to his mother Anne, and the course of English history would have been changed for ever. His death made inevitable a division of loyalties between those who supported the Hanoverian succession and others who wished for continuation of the Stuart line. However, Radcliffe's presence at the prince's bedside, along with his earlier behaviour which had caused Princess Anne to dismiss him, led rise to a satirical poem by Tom Brown who picked on Radcliffe as a scapegoat.

In vain we grieve, in vain we waste our eyes,
And with expostulations rend the skies;
All our complaints we must on Radcliffe spend,
By whose delays more patients sure have dy'd,
Than by the drugs of others misapply'd.
Three bottles keep him, and for their dear sake,
Three bottles unregarded lie at stake.
A saucy humour, thus to over-rate
His pleasure and his ease, to come too late
To such a prince, the hopes of such a state.
Alas!
To throw away some common life's a crime.
That one can ne'er atone for all his time;
But to neglect a life of such a price,
Swells the offence to a much larger size;
In him we all had liv'd; his single fate
Therefore must needs affect the publick state,
So choice a member from the body torn.
Leaves the rest bleeding; for, to say we mourn,
Does not enough express our common grief,
Such as can scarce admit or find relief,
Who can forgive? And yet forgive we must,
For he's the only man that we can trust;
Bewitch'd with apprehensions of his skill.
We thereby give him power and leave to kill.
If by his future care he wou'd retrieve
His fame, and thereby satisfaction give,
Let him, (and 'tis the least that he can do)
His boasted immortalities bestow.

Another of the doctors who attended the Duke in his last illness was William Gibbons who had been at Oxford with Radcliffe and was once foolish enough to say that it was a pity Radcliffe's friends had not made a scholar out of him. In return for this, Radcliffe dubbed him 'Nurse Gibbons' for the way in which he used to treat his patients, a nickname that stuck with him for the rest on his life.

Chapter 6: Other Patients

A long list of Radcliffe's patients in 1712 is to be found in the Radcliffe Science Library, together with the prescriptions he ordered for them. These prescriptions give some idea of his enlightened treatment for patients in comparison to some of the absurd prescriptions of the day. Radcliffe's treatments included Jesuits' bark (quinine) for ague (fevers), and rhubarb and cordials for colic and stomach troubles.

His patients included Sir Isaac Newton, Dr Sharp, Archbishop of York, the Bishops of London and Rochester, and the Duke of Ormonde to whom he later sent a box of medicines for the Duke's use while on campaign in Flanders. For Alexander Pope, the poet, he prescribed 'less study and more exercise',

Jonathan Swift, known as Dean Swift, was another of Radcliffe's patients and became better known as the author of *Gulliver's Travels* than for his position as Dean of St Patrick's Cathedral, Dublin. He spent some years in England, and in his *Journal to Stella* writes, "I still drink Dr Radcliffe's bitter and shall continue it." Dr Radcliffe's bitter sold at Lloyds Coffee House in Lombard Street for one shilling a bottle and was sold as 'a general rectifier of the nerves, head and stomach. It corrects all irregularities of the head and stomach by hard drinking or otherwise'. It is not clear of what its composition consisted!

He recommended many of his patients to take the waters at Bath, and initially was held in high regard in that town. However, he was annoyed by the exorbitant charges of the lodgings and the high cost of housekeepers and so indulged in his customary outspoken

The Radcliffe Observatory

criticisms, leading him to recommend that patients go to the Spa at Tunbridge Wells instead. This caused indignation in Bath, and one citizen published a virulent attack against his skill and arrogant behaviour, saying that, "Such conduct was so sordid and inhuman that no one but one of your base birth and brutish temper could have been guilty of it."

CHAPTER 7: PERSONALITY AND PRIVATE LIFE

In 1704 he moved from Bow Street to a large house in Bloomsbury. The entrance was large, the mantelpieces were of marble, the chairs leather-bound, and the walls adorned with paintings by the great artists of the day including Rembrandt, Rubens and Vandermeer. He had a second smaller house in Hammersmith with a large garden by the Thames, and a third house in Carshalton.

Although he had a reputation in Oxford for being a man of few books, in fact his interests were quite far-reaching, and by the time of his death his library consisted of: 70 folio volumes, typically 15 in (38 cm) in height, the largest sort of regular book; 28 quarto volumes, about 9 in (23 cm) by 12 in (30 cm), roughly the size of most modern magazines; and 111 octavo volumes, about 5 in (13 cm) by 8 in (20 cm), the size of most modern paperbacks. These covered a range of subjects including two Bibles and some volumes of sermons including those of his contemporary, the Dean of St Paul's; medical works by Hippocrates, Willis and Mead, his successor; and volumes by many Greek writers and more contemporary historical and political writings. His library was sold after his death in 1718 to Dr Mead who moved into his house in Bloomsbury Square.

Radcliffe contemplated marriage twice – in 1693 he found a young lady but discovered that she was having a relationship with her wealthy father's bookkeeper, whom she subsequently married – much to her father's displeasure, who would have liked Radcliffe as a son-in-law. When nearly 60 he fell in love with one of his patients but, with his benefactions to Oxford in mind, he said, "Truly he had an old one to think of," and he did not want to share his fortune with another. In his early years his company was sought after by female patients, not solely for medical reasons, as his robust and independent character was attractive to many. He seems to have avoided these advances and once declared that he wished for an Act of Parliament to make it obligatory that women should only be attended by nurses and so leave doctors to attend men.

He fell dangerously ill with pleurisy in 1703, neglected his illness, and drunk a bottle of wine as he took to his bed. It is interesting to note that although he did not frequently bleed his patients, Charles Bernard who attended him took 100 ounces of blood from Radcliffe – that is 2.8 litres or 6 pints, presumably over a number of days. It is not surprising that he was very weak when he "took a strange resolution of being removed to Kensington". At one stage the Queen asked after him, and as he was recovering she was told that he was "ungovernable and observed no rules". Some of the London physicians did not seem to be quite so pleased about his recovery because "those who hoped to share his practice began to think themselves disappointed...".

In 1709 Richard Steele wrote of Radcliffe's reputation in *The Tatler*.

> *You are not so ignorant as to be a stranger to the character of Aesculapius (John Radcliffe) as the patron and most successful of all who profess the Art of Medicine. But as most of his operations are owing to a natural sagacity or impulse, he has very little troubled himself with the Doctrine of Drugs, but has always given Nature more room to help herself than any of her learned assistants, and consequently has done greater wonders than is in the power of Art to perform, for which reason he is half deified by the people and has even been courted by all the world.*

After a serious illness in 1710 he frequently retired to Carshalton and handed over many of his patients to young Richard Mead who was to become his successor. While resident in Bloomsbury,

Radcliffe was said to be making £7,000 per year. He invested in several estates in Wolverton in North Buckinghamshire and at Linton-on-Ouse in Yorkshire, as well as in trading adventures – including the South Seas Trading Company, government loans and lotteries – some of which were successful and some of which were not. He had an extensive wine cellar and entertained lavishly night after night. By 1707 he was worth £80,000.

He was often reluctant to pay small debts and on one occasion a workman who had repaired the pavement in front of his Bloomsbury house caught the Doctor on his doorstep and demanded payment.

"Why, you rascal," said the doctor, "do you pretend to be paid for such a piece of work? You have spoiled my pavement, and then covered it over with earth to hide your bad work." "Doctor," said the workman, "mine is not the only bad work that the earth hides."

The doctor was delighted with the riposte and invited the workman into the house and paid him.

Radcliffe took an active interest in politics, twice becoming a Member of Parliament representing Tory interests – first for Bramber, 1689-95, and then in 1713 he represented Buckingham until his death a year later. However, he did not play a large part in parliamentary affairs and few parliamentary speeches by him are recorded. Nevertheless, there is one passage where he claimed that Parliament had passed regulations to restrain quacks, to the great benefit of the medical profession, and he also went on to defend the doctor who wished to speak on a question of religion and church order, saying, "The business of our calling, which sets before us in a more than ordinary manner the wonderful works of Providence, enables us into as great an insight into Divine speculations as theirs who make no manner of searches into the operations of Nature."

He was a heavy drinker, and was sometimes unwilling to leave taverns when summoned, as the following incident aptly describes:

He was thus deeply engaged at a tavern when he was called on by a grenadier, who desired his immediate attendance on his colonel;

but no entreaties could prevail on the disciple of Aesculapius to postpone his sacrifice to Bacchus (the god of wine-making).

"Sir," quoth the soldier, "my orders are to bring you." And being a very powerful man, he took him up in his arms, and carried him off by force. After traversing some dirty lanes, the doctor and his escort arrived at a narrow alley. "What the Devil is all this?" said Radcliffe. "Your colonel doesn't live here?" "No," said his military friend, "my colonel does not live here – but my comrade does, and he's worth two of the colonel, so by God, doctor, if you don't do your best for him, it will be the worst for you!"

Towards the end of his career Radcliffe is reported saying to Mead, his successor, that as a young physician he possessed twenty remedies for every disease, but at the close of his career he found twenty diseases for which he had no remedy.

One of Radcliffe's close friends in his later years was James Radcliffe, the Earl of Derwentwater, a title bestowed on his grandfather by James II. John Radcliffe claimed a relationship with the Earl of Derwentwater and assumed and used the Earl's coat of arms. The young Earl was grandson of Charles II, nephew of James II and cousin to his son James Stuart. Brought up with the young prince abroad, he returned to England in 1709, as Radcliffe records in a letter to Sir William Swinburne:

"My Lord Derwentwater and his brother and Mr Fenwick are all come safe from Holland and are very well, and we shall drink your health tonight."

The young Earl later took part in the Jacobite rising in 1715, a year after John Radcliffe's death. Surrendering with the Jacobite forces, he was imprisoned in the Tower of London but refused to accept the terms of a pardon to obey the Anglican Church and so was beheaded on Tower Hill.

Chapter 8: Final Days

The last months of John Radcliffe's life were clouded with depression and by the unfair criticism that he had failed to attend Queen Anne on her deathbed as he was too ill. In July 1714 the Queen, although only 50, was seriously ill. She was very stout and apparently Radcliffe had told her previously that she was too fat and ate too much. She appears to have succumbed to acute heart failure which was said to be from eating too many black cherries. She was close to death and had five physicians in attendance, including Richard Mead, and Radcliffe thought there were 'a sufficient number of cooks at the broth'. As she had no surviving heir, the court intrigues revolved around whether to send for James II's son, known now as 'The Old Pretender' or to Germany for the Elector George.

Two hours before the Queen's death, Lady Masham sent for Radcliffe on her own authority, but Radcliffe was ill at his home in Carshalton. As he had no official summons, he wrote saying that the Queen "had always had an antipathy to him, and that his presence would be a disservice to her Majesty and disturb her last moments".

However, when this refusal became known, it was seen by some as disloyalty. He had thus been charged with killing Queen Mary, whom he did attend during her dying illness, and also Queen Anne, whom he did not. So strong were the feelings against the doctor in some quarters for having refused to attend Queen Anne that a group plotted his assassination. Fortunately, however, the plot was made known to him in a letter:

"Doctor – Tho' I am no friend of yours, but on the contrary one that could wish your destruction in a legal way, for not preventing

Oxford and the John Radcliffe Hospital from Hinksey Hill

the death of our most excellent Queen whom you had in your power to save, yet I have such an aversion to the taking away men's lives unfairly, as to acquaint you that if you go to meet the gentleman you have appointed to dine with at the 'Greyhound' in Croydon, on Thursday next you will be most certainly murthered. I am one of the persons engaged in the conspiracy, with twelve more … I am touched with remorse and give you this notice; but take care of yourself lest I repent of it by having it in my power to destroy you, who am your sworn enemy – NG."

Although it may have been a hoax, Radcliffe did not see it in that light and, panic-struck, for a time kept himself a prisoner to his house and local surroundings.

On 31 October 1714 Radcliffe was taken ill in church. He took his own pulse and said that he would die speedily. His prognosis was correct and he died the following day on Monday 1 November at his house in Carshalton, "a victim," said Pittis, his first biographer, "to the ingratitude of a thankless world and the fury of the gout."

Thus died the physician who for a generation was the most trusted consultant in London, who went 'into the regions of eternity, from which he arrested thousands in their passage thither by virtue of his healing prescriptions'.

The Historical Register of 1714 reports his death as follows:

> *Died John Radcliffe, M.D., Member of Parliament for Buckingham, accounted the most eminent Physician this England ever produced. He was a man of good sense, sound judgement, and admirable skill in his art, chiefly founded on the Best Mistress, Experience.*

Carefully embalmed, his body remained at Carshalton for four weeks until his executors decided that Oxford was to be the place of burial. His body was taken from London to Oxford and, at a meeting of the Convocation on 27 November 1714, full directions for the funeral were issued, together with the following injunction (presumably as some still blamed him for the Queen's death) that,

"All Bachelors of arts and undergraduates are commanded to behave themselves in a manner suitable to so solemn an Occasion."

Nothing untoward occurred and the body lay in state in the Divinity school in Oxford on Wednesday 1 December. On Friday 3 December it was carried, by the Bishops of Bristol and Chester, the Master of University College, the Regius Professor of Divinity and the Professor of Law, past Brasenose, Lincoln, Exeter and Jesus Colleges to the Northgate, and back via Carfax to St Mary's Church. Following the service in the University Church of St Mary's, the body was buried in a vault in front of the organ loft on the north of the entrance to the chancel. For over 100 years there was no inscription to commemorate him or mark his tomb, but in 1819 a grave was dug next to Radcliffe's and the plate on Radcliffe's coffin was seen for the first time since his burial.

John Radcliffe
Dr. in Physick
Dyed Nov. 1st
1714 in the 65th year
Of his age.

This inscription was then engraved on the paving stone above his grave.

At a meeting of the Convocation on 16 May 1715 his name was enrolled amongst the benefactors of the University.

His career shows that his greatness was not due to his medical learning but to shrewd diagnosis, a strong personality and practical common sense. He wrote no book or treatise and he added nothing to the history of medical science, yet he was in some respects a reformer and pioneer. He insisted on fresh air in place of closed windows and stuffy rooms. He was opposed to the excessive practice of bleeding which was then almost universally practised. He advocated building up the patient's constitution and had a fond use of blisters and, as another doctor once stated, "It can be said in favour of blisters that patients can rarely be killed by them as (they can) with bleeding, purging and opiates."

Dr James Monro in his Harveian Oration in 1737 said of Radcliffe:

> *So accurate were his diagnoses of present symptoms, so skilful his forecasts of future developments that every patient who was in despair turned his fading eyes on him alone, as one who could remove every cause of sickness and aid the course of events so that the sick man's confidence and the doctor's authority joined forces and conspired together to increase the doctor's reputation.*

Radcliffe's portrait (frontispiece) painted by Kneller, his next-door neighbour in London, now hangs in the Bodleian Library and shows Radcliffe in his full-bottomed wig and his best suit of velvet with yellow buttons. He is shown as having an elevated forehead, hazel eyes and ruddy cheeks, telling of the good cheer of former days, with a double chin, a well-formed nose, and a mouth which generally displayed an agreeable smile.

He died worth £140,000. He had given £40,000 to the University for building an additional library to the Bodleian (the Radcliffe Camera) and to furnish it with books and pay for a librarian. He had also left £5,000 to University College which he had entered as a member on 23 March 1665.

To many of his contemporaries he was not a likeable character. He was monstrously egotistical and self-assertive, he was thrifty to the point of avarice, he might be accused of being neglectful of his less fortunate relations, and – a common failing in his day – he drank heavily and not infrequently to excess. However, these faults were offset by more admirable qualities: a prodigious capacity for work, occasional and unexpected displays of generosity, a rumbustious down-to-earth sense of humour, an ease in conversation which could make him an exhilarating companion, and a capacity for inspiring affection in those whom he chose to be his friends.

Yet despite his conviviality and love of company he was a solitary man. He never married and had no home life with the affections of wife and children. He lost touch with his own family, and apologises for this in his letter to his sister during his last illness. With few friends in the medical profession, he took no part in the Royal College of Physicians. Independent, arrogant and self-assured in his youth, he was yet lonely and cynical with bouts of depression later in life.

Too often Radcliffe was his own worst enemy. His uncompromisingly direct and forceful manor of expressing himself turned many against him. He made few friends among his medical colleagues and was reputedly a difficult member of the Royal College of Physicians. He treated his colleagues with distain, although patients flocked to Radcliffe, flattered to be able to call him their doctor and considered his fee good value for his services.

Perhaps we should leave the final word with Sir William Osler, Regius Professor of Medicine in Oxford at the beginning of the twentieth century, who said of Radcliffe:

> *One lesson learned from his life is that if you do not write, then make money; and, after you finish, leave it (to charity).*

Chapter 9: Radcliffe's Legacy

The Radcliffe Trust

Three centuries after his death, the charitable trust founded by his will of 13 September 1714 still operates as a registered charity. It has given rise to many benefactions but none more so that those institutions and buildings in Oxford which bear his name.

Radcliffe Camera

The Radcliffe Camera (the word 'camera' means simply 'room') was built between 1737 and 1747 with £40,000. The Camera was intended to house a new library with £150 per year for the librarian and £100 per year for the purchase of books. The building was completed in 1747 and the formal opening took place on 13 April 1749 when George Frederic Handel entertained the assembly with vocal and instrumental music.

A statue of Radcliffe by the younger Rysbrack stands over the entrance door to the upper reading room. The Radcliffe Camera is the most prominent and best recognised of all the Oxford buildings that make up the skyline, and caused the English poet, Lionel Johnson, to proclaim:

> *Like to a queen in pride of place, she wears*
> *The splendour of a crown in Radcliffe's dome.*

When Samuel Garth, the physician and poet, heard about Radcliffe's legacy for a library, his comment was that the gift was 'about as logical as if a eunuch should found a seraglio'.

Although John Radcliffe claimed a relationship with the Earl of Derwentwater and assumed and used the coat of arms, the College of Heralds would not confirm this and went so far as to issue an order that the arms were not to be displayed on any building erected from his estate – an order that was ignored by the trustees such that his adopted arms (officially described as a 'bend engrailed sable in a field argent') can be seen in several places, including on the ceiling of the lower room of the Radcliffe Camera, and on the door that links University College quadrangle to the High Street.

In 1851 Henry Acland, a physician at the young age of 35, was appointed as the Radcliffe Librarian. Later to become Regius Professor of Medicine in Oxford, Acland had a vision to build a museum in South Parks in Oxford to advance the teaching of medicine and science. It had support from Sir Robert Peel and William Gladstone who subsequently became Radcliffe trustees. Acland wanted the Radcliffe Library to be part of the museum and in 1856 Acland proposed the library move into the museum and the University have the Radcliffe Camera as a reading room, saying:

> *The Bodleian, overcrowded and greatly expanding, is deficient in a reading room. Dr Radcliffe placed his library designedly close to the Bodleian. Certainly his building could be applied to no more fitting, and no more useful purpose. The literary resources of Oxford would be largely developed, if it became the splendid apartment for the study of the treasures of the university Library.*

In 1860 it was agreed and the museum opened in a historic fashion as the location of the memorable discussion on Darwinism where Professor Huxley did battle with Bishop Wilberforce on the evolution of humanity. The following year Acland supervised the transfer of the library's scientific books to a room in the museum. In 1901 the Radcliffe Science Library was opened adjacent to the museum, and the medical and scientific books were moved to their new home adjacent to the museum.

Radcliffe Observatory 1772

The Observatory building which is now part of Green Templeton College was completed in 1794. Its building was due to the energy of Professor Hornsby, who held the Savilian Chair of Astronomy. He wrote to the Radcliffe trustees in 1768, arguing that he could not carry out his duties as Professor of Astronomy without an observatory and so they agreed to build one. The octagonal tower is based on the Tower of the Winds in Athens, and is surmounted by a globe borne by the figures of Hercules and Atlas. Characters in relief representing the Winds encircle the top of the tower, and signs of the Zodiac encircle the base of the tower.

Until 1839, the Savilian Chair of Astronomy was responsible for the Observatory. Sir Henry Savile, the Warden of Merton College, Oxford, had founded the Chair of Astronomy at the University of Oxford in 1619; he required the professor to observe the skies every night and to record his discoveries.

After 1839 the appointment of George Henry Sacheverell Johnson as an astronomer with no observational experience caused the creation of the new role of Radcliffe Observer. In 1929 the Radcliffe trustees decided to sell the Observatory and erect a new one in Pretoria, partly due to the opinion that the atmosphere in England was unsuitable for some astronomical observations.

At the time of its erection it was one of the largest and best equipped observatories in the world. The Observatory was bought by William Morris, later Lord Nuffield, at a cost of £100,000, for the use of the Medical School and the Nuffield Institute for Medical Research. The Radcliffe trustees granted £65,000 for building the new observatory in Pretoria, and money towards a travelling fellowship in astronomy.

The Radcliffe Camera

The Radcliffe Infirmary

The first proposals to build a hospital for Oxford were made in 1758 at a meeting of the Radcliffe trustees. The sum of £4,000 was released for the new hospital, which was constructed on land given by the Member of Parliament for Oxford, Thomas Rowne. The Radcliffe Infirmary was opened on St Luke's Day 1770 at a final cost of £12,791, three times the estimated cost (which still seems a remarkably familiar story three centuries later). The Bishop of Oxford consecrated the Radcliffe Infirmary's burial ground (long since buried itself), and the congregation prayed that it might be the 'only useless part of the establishment'.

There were just two wards, male and female, but such was the demand by patients that another was opened by the end of the year and three more in October 1771. Such heavy use might seem surprising given the fact that many conditions were barred by the rules. Patients suffering from smallpox (or any infectious disease), epilepsy, ulcers, inoperable cancers, tuberculosis or dropsy were not admitted; neither were pregnant women, children under seven (except for major operations) or the mentally ill.

The honorary physicians and surgeons gave their services free, maintaining themselves by private practice, although there were junior doctors on the paid staff. The hospital depended on voluntary giving, and larger donations conferred the status of Governor, with the right to elect officers and recommend patients. A patient could only be admitted on a Governor's 'turn', a system which was ended officially in 1884. Some of the Governors continued to claim their right to admit patients until 1920, when a tuppence a week Contributory Scheme was introduced. Within three years this was providing 60% of the hospital's income.

In 1939, Professor Howard Florey and a team of researchers at the Sir William Dunn School of Pathology, close to the Radcliffe Infirmary, were experimenting on penicillin and showed the effectiveness of it in mice. On 27 January 1941, the first dose of penicillin was given intravenously to a man at the Radcliffe Infirmary. Due to the short supply of the drug, it was recycled from the patient's urine by Dr Norman Heatley, one of the team involved in the work. With the ongoing war effort, the major production of the drug was carried out in the United States, and at one stage when a German invasion look likely, the researchers put some of the penicillin mould in the inside of their overcoats to make sure that it would still be available and not lost. Fleming, Florey and Chain were awarded the Nobel Prize for Medicine in 1945.

The Infirmary finally closed as a hospital in 2007, having been sold to the University, and whilst the land behind is being redeveloped, the original Grade I listed hospital building will stand unchanged in outward appearance.

University College

By 1687, when Radcliffe's wealth had started to accumulate, he began to cast an eye on 'the fountain from whence it was derived' – namely, University College which he had attended as an undergraduate.

The Radcliffe Quadrangle in University College was completed in 1719. A £5,000 bequest to this college enabled it to build a new quadrangle, with new lodgings for the Master (subsequently transferred to a house in Logic Lane in 1879), and two sets of rooms for the travelling fellows. A figure of Radcliffe as Aesculapius with his staff stands above the entrance gate on the inside of the quadrangle (page 64). In 1687 he presented the East Window of University College, depicting the scene of the Nativity, although this was removed in alterations to the chapel made in 1860.

Travelling Fellowships

He bequeathed an estate in Linton-on-Ouse in Yorkshire to the College to provide the stipends for the two medical travelling fellowships and a Radcliffe Prize of £50 a year. The Radcliffe Travelling Fellowships were awarded so that the most meritorious medical students should be induced to spend several years studying their profession in the great medical centres in Europe, with the hope that they might come back to Oxford. However, soon after they were founded in 1715 Alexander Pope wrote sarcastically that:

Er'e Radcliffe's Doctors travel first to France,
Nor dare to practice till they've learn'd to dance.

JB Nias, himself a travelling fellow, lists in his book on Radcliffe the travelling fellows who were elected from 1715 to 1918. One was David Hartley in 1755 but he never completed his medical degree and resigned his fellowship, entering as a student at Lincoln's Inn in 1759 where he met Benjamin Franklin whose son was also studying there. After becoming Member of Parliament for Hull he spoke persistently against the war with America. When peace was eventually made between Britain and the United States in 1783, Hartley was selected to sign the treaty in Paris as representative of George III while his old acquaintance Benjamin Franklin signed for the United States.

The Napoleonic Wars closed the European schools to the Radcliffe Fellows for thirty years, and James Haworth, elected in 1791, was the first Radcliffe Fellow to go to the United States. Charles Vaughan was elected in 1800 and travelled to various parts of Europe as the wars permitted, but also to Syria and Persia where he undertook various diplomatic roles as well as travelling to Spain at the outbreak of the Peninsular War. He was highly esteemed as a diplomat.

John Wickham was elected a Fellow in 1801 and went to Paris. He was in the unfortunate situation of being there when Napoleon issued orders to arrest all Englishmen found within his dominions and was imprisoned by Napoleon's agents in Paris. Eventually, he was allowed to leave and join a select number of detained persons in Geneva where he enjoyed relative liberty, but wishing to return to England he managed through friends to get Dr Edward Jenner (who pioneered smallpox vaccination) to write to Napoleon. Such was the apparent esteem in which Napoleon held Jenner that Napoleon allowed Wickham to return.

William MacMichael was elected in 1811. He died from a stroke at the age of 55 but not before he had written *The Gold Headed Cane*, referred to earlier. The cane tells its own story as it passes through the hands of five eminent physicians, Radcliffe being the first. It was then deposited in the Royal College of Physicians where it remains to this day.

In 1915 Sir William Osler wrote his introduction to the new edition of the *Gold Headed Cane*, just after the 200th anniversary of Radcliffe's death: "Hoping to have ceremonies appropriate to the 200th anniversary but unfortunately in the midst of the first World War the University had other things to think about."

The Radcliffe travelling fellows continue to this day, one of the more recent being Sir Roger Bannister who, apart from becoming the first man to run a mile in under four minutes at the Iffley Road running track in Oxford in 1954, was an acclaimed neurologist practising in London. He later became Warden of Pembroke College, Oxford. In his day it was to America, rather than Europe, that a young doctor usually wished to travel, collecting the unofficial 'BTA' (been to America) degree after their name. Today the advertisement for the Radcliffe Fellow encourages them to travel to the developing world.

Other grants

Other lesser grants have been made by the Radcliffe trustees to various hospitals and institutions outside Oxford, including St Bartholomew's Hospital and the Royal College of Physicians, both in London. Many grants have been made to ecclesiastical institutions including St John's Church in Wakefield and St Philip & St James Church on the Woodstock Road (a stone's throw north of the Radcliffe Observatory), now the home of the Oxford Centre for Mission Studies.

Nine years after Radcliffe's death, his contemporary Sir Christopher Wren was laid to rest in St Paul's Cathedral. The words written on the stone plaque over Wren's tomb in the crypt of the greatest building he designed could equally well have been written of John Radcliffe with respect to buildings he was responsible for in Oxford.

> *Lector, si monumentum requiris, circumspice.*
> *Reader, if you seek his memorial, look around you.*

Further Reading

Dr John Radcliffe and His Trust, Ivor Guest
(London: The Radcliffe Trust, 1991)

Dr Radcliffe's life and letters: with a true copy of his will and testament, W Pittis
(London: 1716)

The Gold Headed Cane, William MacMichael
(London: Oxford University Press, 1915)

A Book about Doctors, J Cordy Jefferson
(London: Hurst & Blackett, 1860)

Dr John Radcliffe: A sketch of his life with an account of his Fellows and Foundations, JB Nias
(Oxford: Clarendon Press, 1918)

The Life of Dr John Radcliffe, Campbell Hone
(London: Faber & Faber, 1950)

Statue of John Radcliffe, University College

APPENDIX

The Hippocratic Oath

The Hippocratic Oath is an oath historically taken by physicians and other healthcare professionals swearing to practise medicine ethically and honestly. The oath is considered a rite of passage for practitioners of medicine in many countries, although nowadays the modernised version of the text varies among them.

> *I swear by Apollo, the healer, Asclepius, Hygieia, and Panacea, and I take to witness all the gods, all the goddesses, to keep according to my ability and my judgment, the following Oath and agreement:*
>
> *To consider dear to me, as my parents, him who taught me this art; to live in common with him and, if necessary, to share my goods with him; to look upon his children as my own brothers, to teach them this art; and that by my teaching, I will impart a knowledge of this art to my own sons, and to my teacher's sons, and to disciples bound by an indenture and oath according to the medical laws, and no others.*
>
> *I will prescribe regimens for the good of my patients according to my ability and my judgment and never do harm to anyone.*
>
> *I will give no deadly medicine to any one if asked, nor suggest any such counsel; and similarly I will not give a woman a pessary to cause an abortion.*

But I will preserve the purity of my life and my arts.

I will not cut for stone, even for patients in whom the disease is manifest; I will leave this operation to be performed by practitioners, specialists in this art.

In every house where I come I will enter only for the good of my patients, keeping myself far from all intentional ill-doing and all seduction and especially from the pleasures of love with women or men, be they free or slaves.

All that may come to my knowledge in the exercise of my profession or in daily commerce with men, which ought not to be spread abroad, I will keep secret and will never reveal.

If I keep this oath faithfully, may I enjoy my life and practice my art, respected by all humanity and in all times; but if I swerve from it or violate it, may the reverse be my life.

Distemper and the Four Humours

Distemper was term used to refer to the derangement of one of the four humours or 'tempers. The ancient four humours theory may have origins in ancient Egypt or Mesopotamia, but it was the Greek physician Hippocrates (460-370 BC) who developed it into a medical theory. He believed certain human moods, emotions and behaviours were caused by body fluids (called 'humours'): blood, yellow bile, black bile, and phlegm. These latter Galen named respectively 'sanguine', 'choleric', 'melancholic' and 'phlegmatic' after the bodily humours. Each was the result of an excess of one of the humours that produced, in turn, the imbalance in paired qualities. The temperaments are sanguine (pleasure-seeking and sociable), choleric (ambitious and leader-like), melancholic (introverted and thoughtful), and phlegmatic (relaxed and quiet).

John Radcliffe's Letters

John Radcliffe's letter regarding treatment of the Duke of Gloucester

Jul 30-1700

On Sonday the 28.About noon I was sent for to attend upon his Highness the Duke of Glocester at Windsor, and I got thither about six in the evening, where I found his Highness in bed, with a very high feavor upon him, his flesh was extreme hot, a high colour in his cheeks with several eruptions upon his skin and face, attended with a rash which gave som suspicion that it might prove the small pox his puls was very quick and feavourish his tongue white, and his swallowing without paine or difficulty his breathing by fits short and attended with very great and frequent sighing.... And he himself very restless and extreme light-headed.... After that I had inform'd myself of the present circumstances and condition of his distemper – I retird with Dr. Gibbons and Dr. Hanns who were both there before to consult about his recovery before that I came, they had orderd him five blisters which were all put on, wee likewise orderd his Highness a drink to drink of, which was proper to suppress his loosness, which had its effect.... His feavour was a malignant feavour in all its symptoms, with a rash all over the body attending of it. Wee orderd him Cordial powders and Cordial Julops to resist the malignity, he tooke a paper of those powders that night which kept him in breathing sweats and brought out the rash in greater quantity, he had but very little rest that night, accompanied with great sighings and dejection of spirits and towards morning complained very much of his blisters. they were opend in the morning and they were drawn very well and run very well, and upon the running of his blisters he was less light headed and the rash came out the more so that towards noon his head was considerably better, and his breathing freer, which gave us som encouragement at that time to hope his recovery. Wee

orderd him in the evening two more blisters which were apply'd and to continue the method he was in, hopeing by the assistance of them and his other medicins he would have a better night, but before the blisters could take place the malignity of the disptemper retreating from the skin to the vital parts, he was of a suddaine after a litle doseing taken with a convulsive sort of breathing, a defect in swallowing and a total deprivation of all sens which lasted about an hour and between twelve and one that night departed this life.
John Radcliffe